Dance
Of The Raindrops

BY

SARAH DIXON

DEDICATION

Dedicated to the community of
Salapwuk, Pohnpei, Micronesia

The grass is dancing.

The kids are playing.

The thunder is rolling.

The birds are bathing.

The rainbow is blooming.

The Rain is falling.

AUTHOR'S NOTE

While living on the island of Pohnpei in Micronesia, as a Peace Corps Volunteer, I relished the sights and sounds of nature surrounding me. The daily rainstorms could sometimes be heard from a mile away making their way through the lush jungle toward us. This poem was one of many stories that filled my imagination while I worked in the community of Salapwuk as a teacher. Playing in the rain is an idea that brings out the child in all of us. The morning alarm of the birds, the numerous frogs enjoying the moisture and the sound of the rain on the tin roof are just a few of my fond memories. The children of Salapwuk, many of them now grown and some with children of their own, brought me joy every day. Their song, their inventive play, and their connection with the world around them showed me a new way to appreciate life. This book is dedicated to them and the Salapwuk community which opened their arms to me and made me feel like I was one of them.

About the Author

Sarah Dixon is a first grade teacher in Gilroy, California. She lives with her husband, daughter and mother in law in Morgan Hill, CA where she spends her time reading, writing and hiking. She spent her two-year Peace Corps experience on the island of Pohnpei, teaching the children of the small mountain community of Salapwuk.

She hopes to publish many more children's books based on her experiences traveling abroad. Inspired by the languages and cultures of the people she meets and nature that surrounds her, there is no shortage of material. Her vision is that children can enjoy these experiences through her stories as they learn to love reading.

ABOUT THE ILLUSTRATOR

Martha Dixon is a mother, grandmother and former teacher living in Grass Valley, California. She spends her retirement gardening and reading. She still teaches English part time at her local library.